The Complete DASH Diet Book for Beginners

Healthy Recipes for a Weight Loss, Lower Blood Pressure, and Prevent Diabetes

A 14-Day DASH Diet Meal Plan

Dedication:

I dedicate this book to my family, who has always supported me in striving to make our food healthy and tasty.

Contents

Chapter 1. DASH Diet BASICS

What is the DASH Diet?

Dash Diet is the famously known acronym for "Dietary Approaches to Stop Hypertension." As the name indicates, the diet plan was formulated to control hypertension through a dietary pattern. The plan is not purely vegetarian, as many may assume, rather it contains a well-balanced combination of all the nutrients. It consists of low-fat dairy foods, fruits, whole grains, and vegetables. With the idea of controlling blood pressure through minimized fat and sodium intake, experts at the National Heart, Lung, and Blood Institute of United States first promoted "DASH Diet" as an ideal eating plan to prevent and minimize Hypertension.

Health Benefits of the DASH Diet

Though DASH is known to significantly control hypertension, there are many other health benefits which are directly linked to this diet plan and these are:

1. Reduced Hypertension:

DASH is low on salt and sodium content. Thus, it reduces hypertension and keeps the blood pressure in the optimum range. Patients suffering from hypertension are therefore prescribed to the make dietary changes as per the DASH regulations.

2. Weight Loss:

It was not originally formulated to affect body weight, but this healthy plan can serve to prevent obesity. Healthy and controlled diet is linked with better metabolism and lesser fats deposits. So, without cutting out any food in particular, mere maintenance of daily intake through this diet plan can prevent obesity. And people who aspire to lose weight in an effective manner can switch to it to witness fast visible results.

3. Heart Health:

It refers to a healthier heart which results from the diet with lesser fats and complex carbohydrates. Cardiovascular disease is common these days; as the food, we take in is far more concentrated with fats and carbs and low on fibers. This creates clogs in the veins and arteries which results in heart strokes. The DASH diet ensures lesser and controlled intake of all such items, thus preventing all the heart-related diseases.

4. No Osteoporosis:

It is rich in potassium, calcium and proteins hence it prevents the onset of osteoporosis. This disease is unfortunately quite prevalent among women of middles ages or older than that. With a constant intake of this diet plan, the balance of calcium and potassium remains in control.

5. Healthy Kidneys:

It is also a known way to avoid kidney stones which are common due to food with high sodium content. It has no excessive minerals which could deposit in kidneys or dehydrate them. Moreover, better functioning kidneys require a critical balance of sodium and potassium for purification of blood. With lesser sodium intake, this equilibrium remains intact.

6. Diabetes:

A diet which lacks empty carbohydrates can also reduce the number of simple sugars in the blood; resultantly it can help reduce the risk of diabetes. People suffering from type II diabetes suffer from lack of Insulin, the hormone which limits the amount of blood sugar level. This diet, therefore, helps such patients, as it is low on sugars.

7. Prevents Cancer:

It is proven that no treatment can work better than dietary support for cancer patients. As the "DASH" diet is rich in vitamins, fibers, and antioxidants, it consequently helps to prevent the spread of cancer in the body.

The DASH Dietary Program

The DASH dietary program focuses on the different expects of the daily food intake. From the type and form of the ingredients to the total amount and per meal serving. The aim of such a program is to create a workable balance in all the nutrients. Before a person switch to DASH diet, the experts first analyze his or her eating habits, health condition, the rate of metabolism, a sign of ailments and workout routine and then draws out a map towards better health. Like many other dietary programs, DASH is also health oriented, and the basic aim is to achieve the various standards for healthier lifestyles. This may involve prevention of a number of diseases and cure of the others.

Research-Based Benefits of DASH Dieting

Early researches on "Dash Diet" were first conducted by National Institute of Health in the United States. There, the scientists examined three different dietary patterns and documented their results on patients with high blood pressure. The dietary plan which is rich in fruits, vegetables, beans and low-fat dairy products, we now term as "DASH," reduced the Diastolic blood pressure by 3 mm Hg and systolic blood pressure by 6 mm Hg. Statistics also revealed that the diet didn't affect the overall body weight of the patients. It also adjusts the daily caloric intake from 1600 to 3100 dietary calories. "DASH" diet was also tested in the Optimal Macronutrient Intake Trial for Heart Health, and the results from the trial also proved that "DASH" significantly reduces the daily fat intake and consequently prevents hypertension and risk of Heart diseases. Owing to its impact and results, DASH was ranked 1st for "Best Diets Overall" by U.S. News & World Report's Annual Best Diets rankings.

It's a long-Term Solution:

With medicine, you can cure the disease, but only the diet can prevent them in the long run. A healthy diet does not only strengthen us, but also gives us the correct proportion of the nutrients based on the body demand. In this regard DASH has proven itself to be miraculous because it can be subjected to any particular health condition and can suite to any person irrespective of the age and gender. It gives a more generalized perspective of a long-term solution to diseases which are otherwise not completely curable, i.e. cancer, diabetes, and hypertension.

Helps Manage Type 2 Diabetes

Studies have shown that by limiting the caloric intake and reducing body weight, a person becomes more insulin sensitive, which means lesser vulnerability to diabetes. According to the research trials, individuals on the DASH diet showed lower fasting glucose levels in their blood when compared to the individuals who were not. Thus, it is established that restriction on the amount of excessive carbohydrate intake, regularize the insulin function in the body and helps prevent diabetes.

1. It is more flexible:

The broad-ranging option available under the label of DASH diet makes it more flexible for all. This is the reason that people find it easier to switch to it and harness its true health benefits. It makes adaptability easier for its users.

2. Encourages exercise:

It is more effective than other diets because it not only focuses on the food and its intake but it also duly stresses on the daily exercises and routine physical activities. This is the reason that it produces quick, visible results.

3. More inclusive:

With few limitations, this diet has taken every food item into its fold which certain modifications. It rightly guides about the dos and don'ts of all the ingredients and prevents us from those which are harmful to the body and its health.

4. Maintained balance:

One of its biggest advantages is that it maintains the balance in the diet, in our routine, caloric intake, and nutrition.

5. Calories in check:

Every meal we plan on a DASH diet is pre-calculated in terms of calories. We can easily keep track of the daily calories and consequently restrict them easily by cutting off certain food items.

6. No junk food:

It suggests the use of more organic and fresh food and discourages the use of processed food and junk items available in stores. So, it inculcates better eating habits in the users.

7. Preventive in effect:

Though it is proven to be a cure for many diseases, it is described more as a preventive strategy.

8. Allows progress:

The diet is not highly restrictive and accommodates gradual changes towards achieving the ultimate health goal. You can set up your daily, weekly or even monthly targets at your own convenience.

9. Long Lasting results:

The results of the DASH diet are not only incredible but also long-lasting. It is considered slow in progress, but the effects last longer.

10. Activate Metabolism:

With its healthy approach to life, the DASH diet has the ability to activate our metabolism and boost it for better functioning of the body.

Chapter 2. The DASH Diet Weight Loss Breakthrough

How the DASH Diet helps with Weight Loss

Refined starch, carbohydrates, excessive sugars, and fats are all restricted on a DASH diet; this is the reason that it turned out to be a perfect weight loss formula for people of all age. It has a balanced dietary approach, which teaches us to be smarter and more practical about our food preference; instead of omitting certain items, it allows the use of all but in a combination. Instead of refined carbohydrates, it encourages to take more fibrous forms of carbs like whole grains and beans. Same is true for the sugars, where fruit sugars and brown sugars have greater preference over white sugar. Furthermore, the DASH diet also keeps in check the amount of fat in our daily serving, fat-free milk, and plant-based oils effectively aid better weight loss.

DASH Foods and Serving Sizes

One of the defining features of the DASH diet is 'p.' Correct proportions of all the ingredients is the required amount. Excess of everything is best, which sounds true for the DASH Diet. How to determine the proportion is the real question to ask yourself. Based on excessive research and years of studies, experts have come to certain numbers which tell about the amount of the food intake in terms of serving. These figures vary from food type because of the variation of the nutrients they carry. The following table shows serving size of all the major categories of food in a certain caloric diet.

Type of food	Number of servings for 1600 - 3100 Calorie diets	Servings on a 2000 Calorie diet
Grains and grain products (include at least 3 whole grain foods each day)	6 - 12	7 - 8
Fruits	4 - 6	4 - 5
Vegetables	4 - 6	4 - 5
Low fat or non fat dairy foods	2 - 4	2 - 3
Lean meats, fish, poultry	1.5 - 2.5	2 or less
Nuts, seeds, and legumes	3 - 6 per week	4 - 5 per week
Fats and sweets	2 - 4	limited

The Importance of Exercise

Exercise is essential to every active lifestyle. Dietary changes can only prove to be effective when carried out with a daily workout. Exercise aids better digestion, the release of metabolic hormones and catalytic enzymes. It is also quite important for DASH lifestyle.

Exercise helps in burning excess all those calories, help in muscles growth and remove the toxins out of the body. Since DASH is not just a diet but a complete way of life, exercise is equally important for its effectiveness, and it should not be overlooked. This does not mean to opt for strenuous exercises all of a sudden; embrace this change progressively and start with lighter workouts. Activities like cycling, jogging, and playing outdoor physical games can also serve the purpose. 30 minutes daily exercise is advisable to achieve the known benefits of DASH diet. It can include:

- 15 minutes of Walk
- 10 minutes of Running
- 6 minutes of Cycling
- 20 minutes of Swimming Laps
- 60 minutes of Housework

Calorie Needs for Weight Loss

The direct link between food and weight gain can be created through the number of calories we take. This amount should always be according to the body size and energy consumption. Any amount greater than that can cause obesity. This is why we need to maintain our caloric intake for weight loss. The restriction varies from man to man and from woman to man. For average female, the caloric intake should be from 1500 to 2000 calories per day to maintain or lose one pound of the weight. For men, the figure varies from 2000 to 2500 calories

Chapter 3: Decrease Blood Pressure Naturally

Ordinarily known as High Blood Pressure, hypertension is the medical condition where a person suffers from elevated blood pressure in the arteries. For an average adult, the optimum blood pressure must range from 120 mm Hg to 80 mm Hg; any persistent deviation from the normal is considered as hypertension. Among the primary causes of hypertension is the excessive salt intake, obesity, smoking, etc. Thus, by controlling the lifestyle and daily diet, high blood pressure can also be treated and prevented. Foods which are rich in fibers and low on sodium like fruits, vegetables, and nonfat dairy products can prove to be miraculous when it comes to treating hypertension. Without the changes in lifestyle and diet, the cure to hypertension through medication is almost impossible. And the long-term blood pressure disorder can also cause many another fatal disease like atherosclerosis, pulmonary embolism, dementia, heart failure, strokes and ischemic heart diseases.

The short-term effects of incorporating DASH diet into your routine includes controlled blood pressure. If a person is suffering from hypertension, he will experience a decrease of 4 to 3 mm Hg in his diastolic and systolic blood pressures just by following this dietary plan. As the diet is also rich in fibers, it will allow easier digestion and prevents gastrovascular diseases. It also boosts the rate of metabolism in the body, and the person feels physically fit and active. Whereas its long-term impact includes a decreased risk of cardiovascular diseases; prevention of diabetes, obesity, cancer, and kidney stones.

Food Dos and Don'ts

While on DASH diet, excessive fats, salt, and spices need to be avoided. Cut off all the empty carbohydrates from the diet completely, only opt for food which is rich in vitamins, proteins, and fiber.

- **Foods to Enjoy**

It is safe to say that any food can be enjoyed on a DASH diet as long as the balance is maintained. On a broader scale, this diet plan doesn't restrict the use of most of the food items, but it does limit their amount. Following are the list of items which can be enjoyed on a DASH Diet as the given description of the serving size.

1. Grains.
2. Vegetables.
3. fruits.
4. Seeds
5. Nuts
6. low fat or no fat dairy products
7. Beef and pork
8. Poultry
10. Seafood

- **Foods to Avoid**

Food which can cause high blood pressure, hypertension, high blood sugar levels and obesity are all forbidden on a DASH diet. The following list of items should be taken in a lesser amount:

1. Salt
2. Sugary beverages
3. Salted Nuts
4. High fats dairy products
5. Processed food.
6. Excessive animal-based fats

Chapter 4: DASH Diet Frequently Asked Questions

How long does it take for DASH diet to work?
There is no exact time period which can be associated with the results of the DASH diet. The results vary from person to person, with the efforts and the medical conditions of each individual. Normally, it takes a week or two till a person starts feeling its effects from within. And those who are opting it for weight loss can see themselves losing one pound a week provided that the diet and exercise routine is strictly followed.

Is DASH diet a Ketogenic Diet?
Not really; DASH diet is more general and can be molded into any dietary style based on the particular need of a person. It does limit the number of carbohydrates on the daily menu but not up to the extent of a ketogenic diet.

Is the DASH diet suitable for Vegetarians?
It is flexible to various food preferences. Vegetarians can also enjoy the benefits of a DASH diet while keeping up their meat and dairy products aversions. In the DASH diet, there is a number of vegetarian options available which mainly includes grains, fruits, beans, and veggies.

What can we drink on a DASH DIET?
Fresh organic juices with no added preservatives are prescribed on a DASH diet. Avoid fizzy drinks and processed beverages as they contain high traces of sugars. Instead, go healthy and try homemade fruit smoothies to quench your thirst.

BREAKFAST RECIPES:

Millet Congee

Ingredients:
- 8 strips of bacon
- 1 cup hulled millet
- 5 cups water
- 1 cup sweet potato, peeled and diced
- 2 teaspoons ginger, minced
- 1 teaspoon ground cinnamon
- 2 Tablespoons brown sugar
- 1 medium apple, diced with skin
- ¼ cup honey

How to prepare:
1. Sauté bacon in a skillet over medium heat until crispy.
2. Transfer the bacon to a plate lined with paper towel.

3. Mix millet with water, ginger, cinnamon, brown sugar, and sweet potato in a large
   pot.
4. Bring the millet mixture to a boil then reduce the heat to a simmer.
5. Cook for about 1 hour.
6. Turn off the heat and add honey, apple, and bacon crumbles.
7. Garnish with honey and chilies.
8. Serve warm.

Preparation time: 10 minutes
Cooking time: 1hr 5 minutes
Total time: 1 hr. 15 minutes
Servings: 03

Nutritional Values:

- Calories 510
- Total Fat 24.7 g
- Saturated Fat 8 g
- Cholesterol 0 mg
- Sodium 840 mg
- Total Carbs 60.7 g
- Fiber 6 g
- Sugar 41.1 g
- Protein *13.5 g*

Strawberry Breakfast Sandwich

Ingredients:

- 1 tablespoon honey
- 8 ounces low-fat cream cheese, softened
- 1 teaspoon grated lemon zest
- 4 English muffins, split and toasted
- 2 cups (about 10 ounces) sliced strawberries

How to prepare:

1. Blend cheese, zest, and cheese in a food processor.
2. Spread cheese mixture over one half of the muffin.
3. Top them with strawberries.
4. Place the remaining sandwich slices on top.

Preparation time: 5 minutes
Cooking time: 0 minutes
Total time: 5 minutes
Servings: 4

Nutritional Values:

- Calories 316
- Total Fat 14.5 g
- Saturated Fat 8.8 g
- Cholesterol 43 mg
- Sodium 469 mg
- Total Carbs 36.8 g
- Fiber 3.5 g
- Sugar 11.7 g
- Protein 11.2 *g*

Spinach, Mushroom, and Feta Cheese Scramble

Ingredients:
- Cooking spray
- ½ cup fresh mushrooms, sliced
- 1 cup fresh spinach, chopped
- 1 whole egg and 2 egg whites
- 2 tablespoons feta cheese
- Pepper to taste

How to prepare:
1. Sauté mushrooms with spinach in a non-skillet over medium heat for 3 minutes.
2. Whisk egg with egg whites and feta cheese.
3. Pour this mixture into the skillet.
4. Cook for 2 to 3 minutes then flip.
5. Cook for another 1 to 2 minutes.
6. Serve warm.

Preparation time: 5 minutes
Cooking time: 5 minutes
Total time: 10 minutes
Servings: 1

Nutritional Values:

- Calories 435
- Total Fat 13.7 g
- Saturated Fat 12.7 g
- Cholesterol 78 mg
- Sodium 141 mg
- Total Carbs 24.9 g
- Fiber 3.2 g
- Sugar 1.3 g
- Protein 9.2 g

Overnight Oatmeal

Ingredients:
- 4 cups fat-free milk
- 4 cups water
- 2 cups steel-cut oats
- 1/3 cup raisins
- 1/3 cup dried cherries
- 1/3 cup dried apricots, chopped
- 1 teaspoon molasses
- 1 teaspoon cinnamon (or pumpkin pie spice)

How to prepare:
1. Add all the ingredients to a slow cooker.
2. Cook on low heat for 8 to 9 hours.
3. Serve warm.

Preparation time: 05 minutes
Cooking time: 9hrs.

Total time: 9hrs. 5 minutes
Servings: 2

Nutritional Values:
- Calories 346
- Total Fat 15.5 g
- Saturated Fat 0.3 g
- Cholesterol 0 mg
- Sodium 31 mg
- Total Carbs 21.8 g
- Fiber 2.6 g
- Sugar 4.5 g
- Protein 4.1 g

Turkey Sausage and Mushroom Strata

Ingredients:

- 8 ounces wheat ciabatta bread, cut into 1-inch cubes
- 12 ounces turkey sausage
- 2 cups fat free milk
- 1-1/2 cup (4 ounces) reduced-fat shredded sharp cheddar cheese
- 3 large eggs
- 12 ounces egg substitute
- ½ cup chopped green onion
- 1 cup sliced mushrooms
- ½ teaspoon paprika
- Fresh ground pepper to taste
- 2 tablespoons grated parmesan cheese

How to prepare:

1. Set your oven to 400 degrees F.
2. Add the bread pieces to a baking sheet in a single layer.
3. Bake for 400 degrees for 8 minutes.
4. Sauté sausage in a pan for 7 minutes with constant stirring.

5. Mix milk with eggs, parmesan, cheese, paprika, salt pepper and egg substitute.
6. Stir in bread cubes, scallions, sausages, and mushrooms.
7. Transfer the mixture to 13x9 inch baking dish.
8. Cover and refrigerate the dish for 8 hours.
9. Set your oven to 350 degrees F.
10. Bake the casserole for 50 minutes.
11. Slice and serve.

Preparation time: 10 minutes
Cooking time: 60 minutes
Total time: 70 minutes
Servings: 04

Nutritional Values:
- Calories 391
- Total Fat 12.8 g
- Saturated Fat 10.6 g
- Cholesterol 112 mg
- Sodium 32 mg
- Total Carbs 31.5 g
- Fiber 4.2 g
- Sugar 2.5 g
- Protein 7.6 g

Veggie Quiche Muffins

Ingredients:

- 3⁄4 cup low-fat cheddar cheese, shredded
- 1 cup green onion or white onion, chopped
- 1 cup broccoli, chopped
- 1 cup tomatoes, diced
- 2 cups non-fat or 1% milk
- 4 eggs
- 1 cup baking mix
- 1 teaspoon Italian seasoning (or dried leaf basil and oregano)
- 1⁄2 teaspoon salt
- 1⁄2 teaspoon pepper

How to prepare:

1. Set your oven to 375 degrees F. Grease a 12-muffin tray with oil.

2. Add cheese, onions, tomatoes, and broccoli into each muffin cup.
3. Beat all the remaining ingredients in a bowl.
4. Divide this mixture into each muffin cup.
5. Bake for 40 minutes in the oven.
6. Allow it to cool.
7. Serve.

Preparation time: 10minutes
Cooking time: 40 minutes
Total time: 50 minutes
Servings: 4

Nutritional Values:

- Calories 427
- Total Fat 8.6 g
- Saturated Fat 2.1 g
- Cholesterol 4.2 mg
- Sodium 282 mg
- Total Carbs 13 g
- Fiber 1.7 g
- Sugar 2.1 g
- Protein 7.5 g

Fruit-n-Grain Breakfast Salad

Ingredients:

- 3 cups water
- ¼ teaspoon salt
- ¾ cup quick cooking brown rice
- ¾ cup bulgur
- 1 Granny Smith apple
- 1 Red Delicious apple
- 1 orange
- 1 cup raisins
- 1 container (8 oz) low-fat vanilla yogurt

How to prepare:

1. Add 3 cups water to a large pot and boil it over high heat.
2. Stir in bulgur and rice and cook on low heat for 10 mins.
3. Spread the cooked grain on a baking sheet and refrigerate overnight.
4. Toss the mixed grains with all the fruits in a bowl.
5. Stir in yogurt and serve.

Preparation time: 10 minutes
Cooking time: 12 minutes
Total time: 22 minutes
Servings: 02

Nutritional Values:

- Calories 212
- Total Fat 3.9 g
- Saturated Fat 6 g
- Cholesterol 0 mg
- Sodium 135 mg
- Total Carbs 14.3 g
- Fiber 5.4 g
- Sugar 3.3 g
- Protein *5.3g*

CHICKEN RECIPES:

Balsamic Roast Chicken

Ingredients:
- 1 whole chicken, about 4 pounds
- 1 teaspoon dried rosemary
- 1 garlic clove
- 1 tablespoon olive oil
- 1/8 teaspoon freshly ground black pepper
- 8 sprigs fresh rosemary
- 1/4 cup balsamic vinegar
- 1/2 teaspoon brown sugar

How to prepare:
1. Set your oven to 350 degrees F.
2. Rinse and pat dry the chicken.
3. Comvine all the ingredients in a large bowl and rub well on the chicken.

4. Place the chicken in the baking pan and roast for 1hr. 20 minutes.
5. Serve warm.

Preparation time: 10 minutes
Cooking time: 1hr. 20 minutes
Total time: 1hr. 30 minutes
Servings: 06

Nutritional Values:
- Calories 480
- Total Fat 17 g
- Saturated Fat 15.2 g
- Cholesterol 251 mg
- Sodium 456 mg
- Total Carbs 12.1 g
- Fiber 1.1 g
- Sugar 2 g
- Protein 31 g

Spiced-rubbed Chicken

Ingredients:

- 1 cup packed brown sugar
- 16 (about 5 lbs.) skinless, boneless chicken breast halves
- 2 tablespoons paprika
- 2 teaspoons salt
- 2 teaspoons ground coriander
- 2 tablespoons olive oil
- 1 tteaspoon ground black pepper
- 1 teaspoon garlic powder
- 1/2 teaspoons cayenne pepper

How to prepare:

1. Mix all the spices in a bowl.
2. Brush the chicken with oil and rub the spice mixture on it generously.
3. Refrigerate for 15 mins.
4. Heat your oven to 400 degrees F.
5. Bake the marinated chicken for 20 minutes.
6. Serve warm.

Preparation time: 10 minutes
Cooking time: 15 minutes
Total time: 25 minutes
Servings: 8

Nutritional Values:

- Calories 388
- Total Fat 15.2 g
- Saturated Fat 19 g
- Cholesterol 22 mg
- Sodium 572 mg
- Total Carbs 5.4 g
- Fiber 1.2 g
- Sugar 1.3 g
- Protein *27 g*

Mexican Bake

Ingredients:

- 2 (14.5 oz.) cans tomatoes, diced or crushed
- 1 1/2 cups cooked rice, brown
- 1 lb. skinless, boneless chicken breast, diced
- 1 cup frozen yellow corn kernels
- 1 cup chopped red bell pepper
- 1 cup chopped poblano pepper
- 1 (15 oz.) can black beans, drained
- 1 tablespoon chili powder
- 1 tablespoon cumin
- 4 garlic cloves, crushed1 cup shredded reduced-fat Monterey Jack cheese
- 1/4 cup jalapeno pepper slices (optional

How to prepare:

1. Set your oven to 400 degrees F.
2. Layer a 3-quart casserole with rice.

3. Top it with chicken, tomatoes, corn, beans, seasonings, garlic, and peppers.
4. Sprinkle cheese and jalapeno on top.
5. Bake for 45 minutes.
6. Serve warm.

Preparation time: 10 minutes
Cooking time: 45 minutes
Total time: 55 minutes
Servings: 6

Nutritional Values:
- Calories 361
- Total Fat 16.3 g
- Saturated Fat 4.9 g
- Cholesterol 114 mg
- Sodium 515 mg
- Total Carbs 19.3 g
- Fiber 0.1 g
- Sugar 18.2 g
- Protein 33.3 g

Roast Chicken Dal

Ingredients:

- 1 1/2 teaspoons canola oil
- 1 small onion, minced
- 2 teaspoons curry powder
- 1 15-ounce can lentils, rinsed
- 1 14-ounce can diced tomatoes, preferably fire-roasted
- 1 2-pound roasted chicken, skin discarded, meat removed from bones
- 1/4 teaspoon salt, or to taste
- 1/4 cup low-fat plain yogurt

How to prepare:

1. Heat canola oil in a cooking pot over medium heat.
2. Stir in onion and sauté for 4 mins.
3. Mix in curry powder and stir cook for 30 seconds.
4. Add lentils, chicken, salt, and tomatoes.
5. Turn off heat then add yogurt.
6. Serve warm.

Preparation time: 15 minutes
Cooking time: 5 minutes
Total time: 20 minutes
Servings: 4

Nutritional Values:
- Calories 415
- Total Fat 32.7 g
- Saturated Fat 5.1 g
- Cholesterol 4.1 mg
- Sodium 277 mg
- Total Carbs 14.7 g
- Fiber 2.4 g
- Sugar 1.9 g
- Protein 31.2 g

Chicken Kabobs

Ingredients:

- 1pound skinless, boneless chicken breast halves, cut into 1-inch pieces
- 1/4 cup plain low-fat yogurt
- 1 tablespoon lemon juice
- 1 teaspoon dry mustard
- 1 teaspoon ground cinnamon
- 1 teaspoon curry powder
- 1/2 teaspoon salt
- 1/4 teaspoon red pepper, crushed
- 1 large red sweet pepper, diced
- 1 yellow squash, cut into 1/2-inch-thick slices
- Soft pita bread, warmed
- Tomato Relish for garnish

How to prepare:

1. Mix chicken with yogurt, mustard, cinnamon, salt, curry powder, red pepper, and lemon juice in a bowl.
2. Refrigerate for an hour.
3. Preheat the oven broiler.

4. Thread the marinated chicken sweet pepper and squash on the wooden skewers.
5. Grill all the skewers for 5 minutes per side on medium heat.
6. Serve warm with tomato relish.

Preparation time: 10 minutes
Cooking time: 5 minutes
Total time: 15 minutes
Servings: 04

Nutritional Values:
- Calories 345
- Total Fat 16.4 g
- Saturated Fat 9.1 g
- Cholesterol 143 mg
- Sodium 471 mg
- Total Carbs 8.7 g
- Fiber 0.7 g
- Sugar 0.3 g
- Protein 38.5 g

Ginger Chicken with Rice Noodles

Ingredients:

- 2 tablespoons very finely chopped green onion
- 1-1/2 teaspoons grated fresh ginger
- 3 cloves garlic, minced
- 1 teaspoon olive oil
- 1/8 teaspoon salt
- 2 skinless, boneless chicken breast halves
- 2 ounces dried rice noodles
- 1/2 cup chopped carrot
- 1/2 teaspoon finely shredded lime peel
- 1 tablespoon lime juice
- 2 teaspoons olive oil
- 1 to 2 tablespoons snipped fresh cilantro

How to prepare:

1. Mix ginger with garlic, green onion, oil and salt in a bowl.
2. Add chicken and mix well to coat.
3. Place the seasoned chicken on the grill rack and grill for 15 minutes at 170 degrees F.
4. Slice the grilled chicken and set it aside.
5. Cook rice noodles and carrots in boiling water for 4 minutes.
6. Drain and rinse the noodles and carrots.
7. Toss them with lime juice, 2 teaspoon oil, cilantro and lime peel in a bowl.
8. Stir in chicken slices.
9. Serve.

Preparation time: 10minutes
Cooking time: 20 minutes
Total time: 30 minutes
Servings: 4

Nutritional Values:

- Calories 495
- Total Fat 11.5 g
- Saturated Fat 3.8 g
- Cholesterol 183 mg
- Sodium 212 mg
- Total Carbs 10.2 g
- Fiber 1.6 g
- Sugar 0.5 g
- Protein 67.4 g

Creole Turkey Meatballs

Ingredients:

- Nonstick cooking spray
- 1 medium onion, chopped
- 1 medium green sweet pepper, chopped
- 1/2 cup quick-cooking rolled oats
- 1 egg, beaten
- 2 tablespoons fat-free milk
- 2 cloves garlic, minced
- 1 teaspoon dried Italian seasoning, crushed
- 1 teaspoon salt-free seasoning blend
- 1 teaspoon Creole seasoning
- 1 pound uncooked ground turkey

How to prepare:
1. Set your oven to 375 degrees F. Grease a 15 x 10-inch baking dish.
2. Mix onion, oats, milk, egg, garlic, sweet pepper, salt, Creole and Italian seasoning in a bowl.
3. Add turkey and mix well to coat.
4. Make small meatballs out of this mixture.
5. Arrange these balls in the greased pan.
6. Bake for 25 minutes.
7. Serve warm.

Preparation time: 20 minutes
Cooking time: 10 minutes
Total time: 30 minutes
Servings: 06

Nutritional Values:
- Calories 381
- Total Fat 12.9 g
- Saturated Fat 3.5 g
- Cholesterol 37 mg
- Sodium 480 mg
- Total Carbs 9.7 g
- Fiber 1.1 g
- Sugar 1 g
- Protein 25.3g

BEEF AND PORK RECIPES:

Beef Stew

Ingredients:

- 1 pound beef round steak
- 2 teaspoons canola oil
- 2 cups diced yellow onions
- 1 cup diced celery
- 1 cup diced Roma tomatoes
- 1/2 cup diced sweet potato
- 1/2 cup diced white potato with skin
- 1/2 cup diced mushrooms
- 1 cup diced carrot
- 4 cloves of garlic, chopped
- 1 cup chopped kale
- 1/4 cup uncooked barley
- 1/4 cup red wine vinegar
- 1 teaspoon balsamic vinegar

- 3 cups low-sodium vegetable or beef stock
- 1 teaspoon dried sage, crushed
- 1 teaspoon minced fresh thyme
- 1 tablespoon minced fresh parsley
- 1 tablespoon dried oregano
- 1 teaspoon dried rosemary, minced
- black pepper, to taste

How to prepare:
1. Preheat the grill over medium heat.
2. Grill the beef steak for 7 minutes per side then set it aside.
3. Heat oil in a large pot and sauté all the vegetables over medium-high heat for 10 minutes.
4. Dice the grilled steak and add it to the pot.
5. Stir in all the remaining ingredients.
6. Cook for 1 hours on medium-low heat.
7. Serve warm.

Preparation time: 5 minutes
Cooking time: 1hr. 10 minutes
Total time: 1hr. 15 minutes
Servings: 06

Nutritional Values:
- Calories 502
- Total Fat 13.8 g
- Saturated Fat 4.9 g
- Cholesterol 125 mg
- Sodium 587 mg
- Total Carbs 11.1 g
- Fiber 3.1g
- Sugar 0.2 g
- Protein 55.9 g

Vegetable and Beef Skillet

Ingredients:

- 3/4 cup onion, chopped
- 1/2 cup bell pepper
- 1 cup rice, uncooked
- 1 cup tomatoes, chopped
- 1/2 pound lean ground beef
- 1 cup mixed vegetables, chopped
- 2 cups water
- 1/2 tablespoon chili powder
- 1 tablespoon oregano
- 1 teaspoon salt
- 1/2 cup shredded cheese

How to prepare:

1. Sear the beef meat in a nonstick skillet until brown.
2. Stir in peppers and onion. Cook for 10 minutes.
3. Add tomato, water, spices, rice, and mixed vegetables.
4. Bring the mixture to a boil. Reduce the heat.

5. Let it simmer for 20 minutes.
6. Serve with cheese on top.

Preparation time: 6 minutes
Cooking time: 15 minutes
Total time: 25 minutes
Servings: 3

Nutritional Values:

- Calories 318
- Total Fat 14.8 g
- Saturated Fat 3.1 g
- Cholesterol 101 mg
- Sodium 372 mg
- Total Carbs 21.4 g
- Fiber 1.3 g
- Sugar 0.3 g
- Protein 10.2 g

Garlic Lime Marinated Pork Chops

Ingredients:

- 4 (6 ounces each) lean boneless pork chops
- 4 cloves garlic, crushed
- 1 teaspoon cumin
- 1 teaspoon chili powder
- 1 teaspoon paprika
- Fresh black pepper to taste
- Juice of ½ lime (about 1 tablespoon)
- Zest of ½ lime

How to prepare:

1. Season the pork with all the spices, lime juice, lime zest, and garlic in a bowl.
2. Marinate for 20 minutes.
3. Layer the broiler pan with tin foil.
4. Place the seasoned pork in the pan and broil for 5 minutes per side.
5. Serve warm.

Preparation time: 15 minutes
Cooking time: 5 minutes
Total time: 20 minutes
Servings: 4

Nutritional Values:

- Calories 402
- Total Fat 9.8 g
- Saturated Fat 3.4 g
- Cholesterol 22 mg
- Sodium 671 mg
- Total Carbs 21.1 g
- Fiber 3.1 g
- Sugar 0.3 g
- Protein 44 g

Crusted Pork Tenderloin

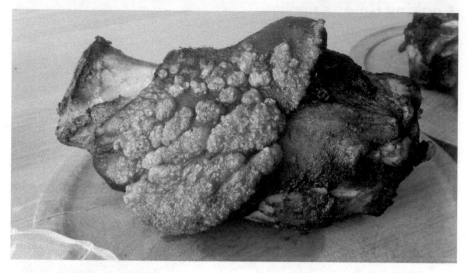

Ingredients:

- 1 pound (16 ounces) pork tenderloin, trimmed of surface fat
- 1 tablespoon canola oil
- 1 tablespoon Cocoa powder, unsweetened
- 1 teaspoon instant coffee
- ½ teaspoon ground cinnamon
- ½ teaspoon chili powder
- Nonstick cooking spray

How to prepare:

1. Set your oven to 400 degrees F.
2. Combine all the spices in a bowl.
3. Season the pork with this mixture along with oil.
4. Heat a greased cast iron pan and add seasoned pork.
5. Cook for 5 minutes per side.
6. Transfer the iron pan to the oven for 15 minutes.
7. Slice and serve.

Preparation time: 10 minutes
Cooking time: 20 minutes
Total time: 30 minutes
Servings: 2

Nutritional Values:
- Calories 511
- Total Fat 24 g
- Saturated Fat 18.5 g
- Cholesterol 49 mg
- Sodium 647 mg
- Total Carbs 26.4 g
- Fiber 1.5 g
- Sugar 1.1 g
- Protein 23.4 g

Asian Beef and Noodles

Ingredients:

- 2 cups water
- 1/2 pound lean ground beef
- 2 packages ramen-style noodles, broken into small pieces
- 1 seasoning packet ramen-style noodles
- 16 ounces frozen vegetables
- 2 green onions, thinly sliced
- 1/4 teaspoon ground ginger
- 2 cloves garlic, minced

How to prepare:

1. Heat a non stick frying pan over medium heat and sauté beef until brown.
2. Stir in 2 cups water and seasoning packet.
3. Add all the vegetables and bring the mixture to a boil.

4. Stir in ramen noodles and cook for 5 minutes.
5. Serve warm.

Preparation time: 10 minutes
Cooking time: 16 minutes
Total time: 26 minutes
Servings: 02

Nutritional Values:

- Calories 411
- Total Fat 10.5 g
- Saturated Fat 2.4 g
- Cholesterol 19 mg
- Sodium 358 mg
- Total Carbs 14.4 g
- Fiber 0.4 g
- Sugar 0.1 g
- Protein 13.4 g

Beef Kabobs with Grilled Pineapple Salsa

Ingredients:

- 1-1/2 pounds beef shoulder center (Ranch) steaks, cut into cubes
- Salt and pepper, to taste

Pineapple Salsa:

- 1 bell pepper, cut into 1 inch pieces
- 1 red onion, cut into 12 wedges
- 1/2 pineapple, peeled, cored, cut into 1-1/2 inch chunks
- 2 teaspoons grated lime peel
- 1/2 teaspoon salt

Marinade:

- 2 tablespoons fresh lime juice
- 2 tablespoons olive oil
- 2 large cloves garlic, minced
- 1 medium jalapeno pepper, minced
- 1/2 teaspoon ground cumin

How to prepare:

1. Slice the beef steaks in small pieces.
2. Season the beef with all the ingredients of the marinade in a bowl.
3. Cover the beef and refrigerate for 30 minutes.
4. Remove the beef from the marinade.
5. Thread the beef on the skewers alternately with vegetables and fruits.
6. Grill the skewers for 15 minutes on a preheated grill.
7. Mix all the ingredients for pineapple salsa.
8. Serve skewers with the salsa

Preparation time: 10minutes
Cooking time: 15 minutes
Total time: 25 minutes
Servings: 4

Nutritional Values:

- Calories 434
- Total Fat 15.6 g
- Saturated Fat 1.1 g
- Cholesterol 11 mg
- Sodium 814 mg
- Total Carbs 23.4g
- Fiber 0.4 g
- Sugar 5.3 g
- Protein 14.6 g

Pork Medallions with Pear-Maple Sauce

Ingredients:

- 1 12- to 16-ounce pork tenderloin
- 2 teaspoons snipped fresh rosemary
- 1 teaspoon snipped fresh thyme
- 1/4 teaspoon black pepper
- 1 tablespoon olive oil or cooking oil
- 2 medium pears, peeled and coarsely chopped
- 1/4 cup pure maple syrup
- 2 tablespoons dried tart red cherries, halved
- 2 tablespoons dry white wine
- 1/4 teaspoon salt

How to prepare:

1. Slice the meat and mix with salt, pepper, thyme, and rosemary in a bowl.
2. Heat cooking oil in a skillet and add meat to sear until brown.
3. Stir in all the remaining ingredients and cook for 3 minutes.
4. Serve warm.

Preparation time: 5 minutes
Cooking time: 5 minutes
Total time: 10 minutes
Servings: 2

Nutritional Values:
- Calories 318
- Total Fat 3.8 g
- Saturated Fat 0.7 g
- Cholesterol 22 mg
- Sodium 620 mg
- Total Carbs 28.3 g
- Fiber 2.4 g
- Sugar 1.2 g
- Protein 5.4g

SEAFOOD RECIPES:

Spicy Seafood Stew

Ingredients:
- 8 ounces fresh skinless fish fillets, cut into pieces
- 6 ounces fresh shrimp, peeled and deveined
- 2 teaspoons olive oil
- 2/3 cup chopped onion
- 1/2 cup finely chopped carrot
- 1/2 cup red pepper, chopped
- 2 cloves garlic, minced
- 1 14-1/2-ounce can low-sodium tomatoes, undrained and cut up
- 1 8-ounce can low-sodium tomato sauce
- 1 cup reduced-sodium chicken broth
- 1/4 cup red wine
- 2 bay leaves
- 1 tablespoon snipped fresh thyme

- 1/2 teaspoon Cajun seasoning
- 1/4 teaspoon ground cumin
- 1/4 teaspoon crushed red pepper

How to prepare:
1. Heat 2 tsp oil in a cooking pot and add onion, garlic, carrot, and sweet pepper.
2. Sauté for 5 minutes then add tomato sauce, broth, wine, tomatoes, bay leaves, dried thyme, cumin, red pepper and Cajun seasoning.
3. Bring cajun mixture to a boil and cook for 20 minutes at a low simmer.
4. Add fresh thyme and seafood.
5. Cover the lid and cook for 5 minutes.
6. Serve warm.

Preparation time: 15 minutes
Cooking time: 25 minutes
Total time: 35 minutes
Servings: 04

Nutritional Values:
- Calories 298
- Total Fat 5.7 g
- Saturated Fat 1.7 g
- Cholesterol 15 mg
- Sodium 394 mg
- Total Carbs 12.4 g
- Fiber 0.2g
- Sugar 0 g
- Protein 16.9 g

Shrimp Pasta Primavera

Ingredients:

- 1-1/4 cup fresh asparagus, sliced into 1-inch lengths (about 1/2 pound)
- 1 tablespoon garlic, minced
- 12 ounces whole wheat penne pasta
- 1/2 cup green onion, sliced thinly
- 1 cup green peas, fresh or frozen
- 2 teaspoons olive oil
- 1/8 teaspoon red pepper, crushed
- 2 teaspoons fresh lemon juice
- 1 tablespoon fresh parsley, chopped
- 1/3 cup grated Parmesan cheese
- 1 lb. shrimp, peeled and deveined
- 1/2 teaspoons salt
- Fresh ground black pepper

How to prepare:

1. Boil water in a 6-quart pot and add asparagus and peas for 4 minutes.
2. Drain and rinse then set them aside.
3. Cook pasta as per the given instructions on the box.
4. Drain and rinse the pasta.
5. Heat oil in a skillet and add garlic and red pepper.
6. Cook for 1 minute then adds shrimp.
7. Sauté for 2 minutes per side.
8. Stir in all the remaining ingredients.
9. Cook for 4 to 5 minutes.
10.   Serve warm.

Preparation time: 5 minutes
Cooking time: 15 minutes
Total time: 20 minutes
Servings: 4

Nutritional Values:

- Calories 249
- Total Fat 11.9 g
- Saturated Fat 1.7 g
- Cholesterol 78 mg
- Sodium 79 mg
- Total Carbs 1.8 g
- Fiber 1.1 g
- Sugar 0.3 g
- Protein 35 g

Poached Salmon with Mustard-Dill Sauce

Ingredients:

- 1 1/2 teaspoons cornstarch
- 1 tablespoons lemon juice
- Black pepper to taste
- 2 teaspoons Dijon mustard
- 1 teaspoon olive
- 2 tablespoons fresh dill, chopped
- 1/4 cup reduced-fat sour cream
- 1 1/4 lb. salmon fillet, cut into 4 portions
- 2 tablespoon shallots, finely chopped
- 1 1/2 cup fat-free milk
- 1/2 teaspoon salt

How to prepare:

1. Preheat oil in a 10-inch skillet over medium heat.

2. Add shallots and sauté for 1 minute.
3. Stir in milk, salt, and pepper. Bring the mixture to a simmer.
4. Add salmon pieces and cook for 10 to 12 minutes.
5. Transfer the fish to a plate using a slotted spoon.
6. Cover fish with foil and set it aside.
7. Mix lemon juice with cornstarch in a bowl.
8. Pour this slurry into the skillet and cook for 1 minute.
9. Stir in dill, mustard, and sour cream.
10.   Pour this sauce over cooked fish.
11.   Garnish with fresh and sautéed vegetables of your choice.
12.   Serve warm.

Preparation time: 15 minutes
Cooking time: 15 minutes
Total time: 30 minutes
Servings: 2

Nutritional Values:
- Calories 301
- Total Fat 12.2 g
- Saturated Fat 2.4 g
- Cholesterol 110 mg
- Sodium 276 mg
- Total Carbs 15 g
- Fiber 0.9 g
- Sugar 1.4 g
- Protein 28.8 g

Grilled Pesto Shrimp Skewers

Ingredients:

- 1 cup fresh basil leaves, chopped
- 1 clove garlic, peeled
- ¼ cup grated Parmigiano Reggiano cheese
- 3 tablespoons olive oil
- 1 ½ pounds jumbo shrimp, peeled and deveined
- Salt and pepper to taste
- 7 wooden skewers

How to prepare:

1. Chop basil with garlic, parmesan cheese, pepper, and salt in a food processor.
2. Add this mixture to the shrimp and mix well to a coat.
3. Marinate shrimp for 2 to 3 hours in the refrigerator.
4. Thread the shrimp over wooden skewers.
5. Heat a grill over medium-low heat. Grease its grilling grate with oil.

6. Grill each skewer for 4 minutes per side.
7. Serve warm.

Preparation time: 10 minutes
Cooking time: 10 minutes
Total time: 20 minutes
Servings: 2

Nutritional Values:
- Calories 348
- Total Fat 12.4 g
- Saturated Fat 0.1 g
- Cholesterol 320 mg
- Sodium 350 mg
- Total Carbs 12.2 g
- Fiber 0.7 g
- Sugar 0.7 g
- Protein 44.3 g

Shrimp Scampi

Ingredients:

- 1 tablespoon basil leaves, minced
- 4 tablespoons butter
- 2 teaspoons red pepper flakes
- 1 tablespoon lemon juice
- 1 teaspoon dried chives
- 1 tablespoon minced garlic
- 2 tablespoons vegetable stock
- 1 lb defrosted shrimp

How to prepare:

1. Melt butter in a 6-inch skillet over medium heat
2. Stir in garlic and red pepper flakes to sauté for 2 minutes.
3. Add the remaining ingredients to the pan.
4. Cook for 5 minutes with occasional stirring.
5. Let the shrimp rest for 1 minute.
6. Mix gently and garnish with basil.
7. Serve warm.

Preparation time: 5 minutes
Cooking time: 8 minutes
Total time: 13 minutes
Servings: 04

Nutritional Values:

- Calories 372
- Total Fat 11.1 g
- Saturated Fat 5.8 g
- Cholesterol 610 mg
- Sodium 749 mg
- Total Carbs 0.9 g
- Fiber 0.2 g
- Sugar 0.2 g
- Protein 63.5 g

Broiled Halibut with Tangy Yogurt Sauce

Ingredients:

- 2 (5 ounces) halibut fillets
- 1 cup nonfat plain yogurt
- 1 large clove garlic, peeled and crushed
- ¼ teaspoon ground black pepper
- ¼ cup freshly squeezed lemon juice
- ¼ teaspoon salt

How to prepare:

1. Preheat your oven broiler.
2. Mix lemon juice with yogurt, garlic, pepper, and salt in a bowl.
3. Line a broiler pan with foil.
4. Place the fish fillets on the pan.
5. Pour half of the yogurt mixture on top of the fish.
6. Broil for 10 minutes.

7. Serve warm with remaining yogurt sauce.
8. Garnish with chopped scallions.
9. Enjoy.

Preparation time: 15 minutes
Cooking time: 10 minutes
Total time: 25 minutes
Servings: 2

Nutritional Values:
- Calories 427
- Total Fat 13.5 g
- Saturated Fat 3.5 g
- Cholesterol 112 mg
- Sodium 342 mg
- Total Carbs 6.6g
- Fiber 0.2 g
- Sugar 0.1 g
- Protein 22.5 g

Sweet Pepper Salsa Fish

Ingredients:

- 1 pound skinless fish fillets (3/4 inch thick)
- 2 tablespoons cooking oil
- 1-1/2 cups fresh mushrooms, quartered
- 1 cup coarsely chopped sweet pepper
- 1 small onion, halved and sliced
- 1 cup salsa
- Fresh oregano (optional)

How to prepare:

1. Heat a tablespoon cooking oil in a pan and add all the vegetables along with mushrooms.
2. Sauté for 5 minutes then transfer to a plate.
3. Add remaining oil to the skillet and sear the fish fillets for 5 minutes per side.
4. Add cooked vegetables and salsa on top.
5. Cook for 2 minutes on low heat.

6. Garnish with oregano.
7. Serve warm.

Preparation time: 10 minutes
Cooking time: 15 minutes
Total time: 25 minutes
Servings: 03

Nutritional Values:
- Calories 313
- Total Fat 8.5 g
- Saturated Fat 2.1 g
- Cholesterol 21 mg
- Sodium 397 mg
- Total Carbs 5.4 g
- Fiber 0.2 g
- Sugar 0 g
- Protein 20.1g

VEGETARIAN RECIPES

Apricot & Spinach Quinoa

Ingredients:

- 1 cup quinoa
- 2 teaspoons extra-virgin olive oil
- 2 cloves garlic, minced
- 1/2 cup dried apricots, coarsely chopped
- 2 cups water
- 1/4 teaspoon salt
- 2/3 cup Moroccan-Spiced Lemon Dressing, divided
- 1 cup cherry tomatoes, halved
- 1 small red onion, chopped
- 8 cups baby spinach
- 1/4 cup sliced almonds, toasted

How to prepare:

1. Add quinoa to a skillet and sauté for 5 minutes.

2. Pass it through a sieve then rinse well.
3. Heat oil in a saucepan over medium heat.
4. Stir in garlic and sauté for 1 minute.
5. Add quinoa and apricots. Stir while cooking for 4 minutes.
6. Stir in water along with salt and bring it to a boil
7. Reduce the heat and cook for 18 minutes.
8. Mix the cooked quinoa with half of the lemon dressing.
9. Allow it to cool for 10 minutes.
10. Stir in tomatoes, onion, and remaining dressing.
11. Divide the spinach leaves into four platters.
12. Spoon the quinoa mixture on top.
13. Serve.

Preparation time: 15 minutes
Cooking time: 20 minutes
Total time: 25 minutes
Servings: 04

Nutritional Values:
- Calories 198
- Total Fat 6.7 g
- Saturated Fat 3.7 g
- Cholesterol 15 mg
- Sodium 124 mg
- Total Carbs 9.4 g
- Fiber 0g
- Sugar 0 g
- Protein 4.9 g

Tomato Pappardelle

Ingredients:

- 8 plum tomatoes, halved lengthwise
- 3 tablespoons olive oil
- Salt and freshly ground black pepper
- 12 ounces pappardelle or Mafalda pasta
- 1 clove garlic, minced
- 1 8-ounce can tomato sauce
- 1 tablespoon snipped fresh thyme
- 1/4 teaspoon crushed red pepper
- 1/4 teaspoon freshly ground black pepper
- 1/4 cup coarsely shaved pecorino Romano cheese

How to prepare:

1. Set your oven to 450 degrees F.
2. Layer a 15 x 10-inch baking pan with tin foil.
3. Place tomatoes in the pan and add 1 tablespoon oil, salt, and pepper on top.

4. Roast them for 20 to 25 minutes then cut them in half.
5. Cook pasta as per given instructions on the box.
6. Rinse and drain then set it aside.
7. Heat the remaining oil in a saute pan and add garlic to sauté for 30 seconds.
8. Add tomato sauce, thyme, and red pepper.
9. Let it boil then reduce the heat.
10. Let it simmer for 2 minutes then add roasted tomatoes, pasta, and black pepper.
11. Garnish with cheese.
12. Serve.

Preparation time: 10 minutes
Cooking time: 30 minutes
Total time: 40 minutes
Servings: 4

Nutritional Values:

- Calories 449
- Total Fat 8.9 g
- Saturated Fat 3.7 g
- Cholesterol 18 mg
- Sodium 119 mg
- Total Carbs 7.8 g
- Fiber 1.6 g
- Sugar 2.1 g
- Protein 15 g

Minted Peas Feta Rice

Ingredients:
- 3/4 cup sliced scallions
- 1 1/4 cups vegetable broth
- 3/4 cup brown rice
- 1 1/2 cups frozen peas
- 1/4 cup sliced fresh mint
- 1/4 cup finely crumbled feta cheese
- Freshly ground pepper, to taste

How to prepare:
1. Boil broth in a saucepan over medium heat.
2. Add rice and bring it to a simmer. Cook for 4 minutes.
3. Stir in peas and cook for 6 minutes.
4. Turn off the heat then add feta, mint, scallions, and pepper.
5. Serve warm.

Preparation time: 15 minutes
Cooking time: 10 minutes
Total time: 25 minutes
Servings: 2

Nutritional Values:

- Calories *281*
- Total Fat 18.2 g
- Saturated Fat 7.4 g
- Cholesterol 110 mg
- Sodium 516 mg
- Total Carbs 10.3 g
- Fiber 1.9 g
- Sugar 0.7 g
- Protein 8.8 g

Grilled Vegetables on Focaccia

Ingredients:

- 3 tablespoons balsamic vinegar or wine vinegar
- 2 tablespoons water
- 1 tablespoons olive oil
- 1 teaspoon dried oregano, crushed
- 2 large red and/or orange sweet peppers
- 2 medium zucchinis, sliced
- 1 medium eggplant, cut crosswise into 1/2-inch slices
- 2 ounces soft goat cheese (Chevre)
- 2 ounces fat-free cream cheese
- 1 purchased focaccia (about a 12-inch round)
- Fresh oregano (optional)

How to prepare:

1. Mix oregano with water, oil, and vinegar in a bowl.
2. Cut the sweet peppers in quarter pieces.
3. Remove the stems and the seeds.

4. Place the vegetables on the grilling rack and coat them with vinegar mixture.
5. Grill for 10 minutes on medium heat while turning constantly.
6. Mix cream cheese with goat cheese in a bowl.
7. Slice focaccia into 4 pieces.
8. Top each piece with cheese mixture and grilled vegetables.
9. Garnish with oregano.
10.   Serve warm.

Preparation time: 10 minutes
Cooking time: 10 minutes
Total time: 20 minutes
Servings: 4

Nutritional Values:
- Calories 348
- Total Fat 4.4 g
- Saturated Fat 2.1 g
- Cholesterol 10 mg
- Sodium 350 mg
- Total Carbs 31.2 g
- Fiber 2.7 g
- Sugar 0.6 g
- Protein 7.3 g

Mediterranean Vegetables

Ingredients:
- ¼ cup cherry tomatoes
- 1 large courgette
- 1 green pepper, chopped
- 1 large parsnip, sliced
- 1 medium carrot, sliced
- 1 teaspoon mixed herbs
- 2 tablespoons honey
- 1 teaspoon mustard
- 2 teaspoons garlic puree
- 6 tablespoons olive oil
- Salt and pepper

How to prepare:
1. Preheat oven to 270 degrees F.

2. Add parsnip, green pepper, zucchinis, carrot, and cherry tomatoes to a baking sheet.
3. Stir in olive and toss well to coat.
4. Roast the veggies for 15 minutes
5. Combine all the remaining ingredients in a bowl.
6. Toss in the roasted vegetable mixture.
7. Whisk well and return the mixture to the baking sheet.
8. Bake for 5 minutes.
9. Serve.

Preparation time: 5 minutes
Cooking time: 20 minutes
Total time: 25 minutes
Servings: 04

Nutritional Values:
- Calories 372
- Total Fat 11.1 g
- Saturated Fat 5.8 g
- Cholesterol 610 mg
- Sodium 749 mg
- Total Carbs 0.9 g
- Fiber 0.2 g
- Sugar 0.2 g
- Protein 63.5 g

Cauliflower Veggie Burger

Ingredients:

- 3 large eggs
- 3 cups cauliflower florets
- ½ cup almond flour
- 3 tablespoons coconut flour
- 1 teaspoon coconut oil (melted)
- ½ teaspoon garlic powder
- ½ teaspoon turmeric
- ½ teaspoon parsley
- Salt and pepper to taste
- Cooking oil spray

How to prepare:

1. Set your oven to 375 degrees F.
2. Finely chop cauliflower in a food processor.

3. Mix cauliflower rice with almond flour, parsley, coconut flour, garlic
      powder, turmeric, and parsley in a large bowl.
4. Whisk eggs with coconut oil in a bowl.
5. Add this egg mixture to the cauliflower rice.
6. Toss well and male 4 butter patties using ¼ cup of this mixture for each.
7. Arrange the burger patties in a greased baking pan.
8. Drizzle some oil on top.
9. Bake for about 30 minutes at 375 degrees F.
10.   Serve warm with lettuce leaves.

Preparation time: 5 minutes
Cooking time: 30 minutes
Total time: 35 minutes
Servings: 4

Nutritional Values:
- Calories 127
- Total Fat 3.5 g
- Saturated Fat 0.5 g
- Cholesterol 162 mg
- Sodium 142 mg
- Total Carbs 3.6g
- Fiber 0.4 g
- Sugar 0.5 g
- Protein 21.5 g

Farfalle with Mushrooms and Spinach

Ingredients:
- 6 ounces dried farfalle (bow-tie pasta)
- 1 tablespoon olive oil
- 1 medium onion, chopped
- 1 cup sliced Portobello
- 2 cloves garlic, minced
- 4 cups thinly sliced fresh spinach, chopped
- 1 teaspoon snipped fresh thyme
- 1/8 teaspoon pepper
- 2 tablespoons shredded Parmesan cheese

How to prepare:
1. Cook farfalle pasta as per the given instructions on the box.
2. Rinse and drain well. Set it aside.
3. Heat oil in a skillet and add onion, garlic, and mushrooms.

4. Cook for 3 minutes then stir in pepper, thyme, and spinach.
5. Sauté for 1 minutes. Add pasta and mix well.
6. Add cheese on top.
7. Serve warm.

Preparation time: 10 minutes
Cooking time: 5 minutes
Total time: 15 minutes
Servings: 04

Nutritional Values:

- Calories 313
- Total Fat 7.5 g
- Saturated Fat 1.1 g
- Cholesterol 20 mg
- Sodium 97 mg
- Total Carbs 21.4 g
- Fiber 0 g
- Sugar 0 g
- Protein 5.1g

LEGUMES AND GRAINS RECIPES

Red Bean Soup

Ingredients:
- 6 cups water
- 1 pound dry red kidney beans

For soup
- 8 cups water
- 3/4 cup dry white wine
- 1 onion, chopped
- 1 tomato, chopped
- 4 cloves garlic, minced
- 1 green or red sweet pepper, chopped
- 1 medium fresh yellow wax chile pepper
- 1 pound beef brisket, trimmed of fat and cut into 3/4-inch pieces
- 1 ham hock
- 1 large russet potato, peeled and diced
- 1 teaspoon salt
- 1/2 teaspoon ground black pepp

How to prepare:

1. Fill a large pot with 6 cups of water along with beans. Let it boil.
2. Cover the lid and cook for 1 hours.
3. Drain and rinse the beans.
4. Add 8 cups water, broth, beef brisket, ham hock, onion, tomato, garlic, chile pepper, beans and sweet pepper to a large saucepan.
5. Boil this mixture then reduce its heat.
6. Put the lid and cook for 1.5 hours.
7. Remove the ham hock and mash the beans using a spoon.
8. Stir in potato and again boil the mixture. Cover the lid.
9. Let it simmer for 15 minutes.
10. Remove bones from the ham and cut it into cubes.
11. Return the ham to the pot.
12. Adjust seasoning with salt and pepper.
13. Serve warm

Preparation time: 10 minutes
Cooking time: 3hrs. 5minutes
Total time: 3hrs 15 minutes
Servings: 06

Nutritional Values:

- Calories 540
- Total Fat 12.5 g
- Saturated Fat 12.7 g
- Cholesterol 13 mg
- Sodium 1474 mg
- Total Carbs 27.3 g
- Fiber 0g
- Sugar 0 g
- Protein 24.1 g

Black-Eyed Peas

Ingredients:

- 2 ounces cooked, smoked lean ham, diced
- 1 onion, chopped
- 1 (14-1/2-oz.) can diced tomatoes
- Salt, to taste
- 1 carrot, thinly sliced
- 8 oz. black-eyed peas, dried
- 1 serrano pepper, seeded and thinly
- 6 cups water, divided

How to prepare:

1. Add peas and water to a saucepan.
2. Boil the water then reduce the heat.
3. Let it simmer for 2 minutes.
4. Turn the heat off and cover the lid. Let it stay for 1 hour.
5. Drain peas and transfer them to the saucepan

6. Add 2 cups water, onion, salt, ham, carrot and serrano pepper.
7. Bring the pepper mixture to a boil then reduce the heat.
8. Cover the lid and let it simmer for 1 hour.
9. Add tomatoes and again boil the mixture.
10.   Let it simmer for 5 minutes.
11.   Serve warm.

Preparation time: 10 minutes
Cooking time: 2hrs. 10 minutes
Total time: 2hrs. 20 minutes
Servings: 6

Nutritional Values:

- Calories 629
- Total Fat 17.5 g
- Saturated Fat 10.7 g
- Cholesterol 68 mg
- Sodium 763 mg
- Total Carbs 19.9 g
- Fiber 1.3 g
- Sugar 0.6 g
- Protein 9.3 g

Ingredients:

- 4 (4 oz.) boneless, skinless chicken breasts
- 1 cup onion, chopped
- 1 cup diced fresh green bell peppers
- 1 1/2 cup low sodium chicken broth
- 1/2 cup fat free half and half milk
- 2 (15 oz.) white cannellini beans, drained and rinsed
- 2 - 3 tablespoons. Chipotle Seasoning Blend

How to prepare:

Add onions and peppers to a saucepan and sauté for 2 minutes.

1. Stir in broth and a half and half milk. Cook for 2 minutes.
2. Grill chicken pieces for 3 minutes per side.
3. Dice the grilled chicken into cubes.
4. Add cannellini beans, chicken, and creole seasoning blend to the onion mixture.
5. Mix well and cook for 1 minute.
6. Serve warm.

Preparation time: 05 minutes
Cooking time: 10 minutes
Total time: 15 minutes
Servings: 4

Nutritional Values:

- Calories 437
- Total Fat 8.8 g
- Saturated Fat 1.2 g
- Cholesterol 0.5 mg
- Sodium 739 mg
- Total Carbs 25.3 g
- Fiber 3.9 g
- Sugar 0.5 g
- Protein 11.8 g

Sweet Potato & Lentil Soup

Ingredients:

- 2 teaspoons medium curry powder
- 3 tablespoons olive oil
- 2 onions, grated
- 1 apple, peeled, cored and grated
- 3 garlic cloves, crushed
- 2 tablespoons coriander, stalks chopped
- thumb-size piece fresh root ginger, grated
- 2/3 lb. sweet potatoes
- 5 cups vegetable stock
- ½ cup brown lentils
- 1.3 cups milk
- juice 1 lime

How to prepare:

1. Toast the curry powder in a saucepan for 2 minutes on medium heat.

2. Stir in olive oil and cook until sizzles.
3. Add apple, garlic, coriander, ginger, and onions to the pan.
4. Cook for 5 minutes with constant stirring.
5. Whisk all the remaining ingredients and cover the lid.
6. Cook for 20 minutes.
7. Serve warm.

Preparation time: 10 minutes
Cooking time: 30 minutes
Total time: 40 minutes
Servings: 6

Nutritional Values:

- Calories 426
- Total Fat 13.1 g
- Saturated Fat 9.1 g
- Cholesterol 14 mg
- Total Carbs 14.4 g
- Sugar 1.2 g
- Fiber 3.8 g
- Sodium 326 mg
- Protein *6.3 g*

Smoked Mackerel, Orange & Couscous

Ingredients:

- ¼ cup couscous
- 2 oranges , peeled and thinly sliced
- Juice from 1 orange
- 3 tablespoons red wine vinegar
- 1 teaspoon sugar
- 3 tablespoons olive oil
- 1 red onion , finely chopped
- ½ cup watercress, roughly chopped
- ½ lb. pack peppered mackerel fillets, flaked into large chunks

How to prepare:

1. Add couscous to the boiled water and let it stay for 10 minutes.
2. Drain and fluff it with a fork.
3. Mix the remaining ingredients in a bowl.

4. Transfer the couscous to the bowl and mix well.
5. Serve.

Preparation time: 10 minutes
Cooking time: 10 minutes
Total time: 20 minutes
Servings: 02

Nutritional Values:

- Calories 215
- Total Fat 9.4 g
- Saturated Fat 2.5 g
- Cholesterol 0.4 mg
- Total Carbs 13.4 g
- Sugar 3.1 g
- Fiber 1.2 g
- Sodium 310 mg
- Protein *5.6 g*

Curried Vegetable Couscous

Ingredients:

- 1/2 yellow onion, coarsely chopped
- 1 celery stalk, cut into 1-inch pieces
- 1/2 carrot, peeled and diced
- 1/3-inch ginger, sliced
- 1 tablespoon extra-virgin olive oil
- 1 garlic clove, minced
- 1 teaspoon curry powder
- 1/2 red bell pepper, chopped
- 1 cup whole-wheat couscous
- 2 cups low-sodium vegetable stock or broth
- 2 tablespoons chopped fresh cilantro

How to prepare:
1. Coarsely chop all the vegetables in food processor.

2. Heat oil in a skillet and all the chopped vegetables.
3. Sauté for about 3 minutes then stir in curry powder.
4. Cook for 1 minute then add couscous and stock.
5. Bring the couscous mixture to a boil then reduce the heat.
6. Cover the pan and cook for 5 minutes.
7. Turn off the heat then toss in cilantro.
8. Serve warm.

Preparation time: 10 minutes
Cooking time: 10 minutes
Total time: 20 minutes
Servings: 4

Nutritional Values:

- Calories 324
- Total Fat 7.4 g
- Saturated Fat 7.1 g
- Cholesterol 10 mg
- Total Carbs 15.4 g
- Sugar 0.7 g
- Fiber 2.8 g
- Sodium 536 mg
- Protein 6.2 g

Curried Squash, Lentil & Coconut Soup

Ingredients:

- 1 tablespoon olive oil
- 1 butternut squash, peeled, deseeded and diced
- 1 cup carrots, diced
- 1 tablespoon curry powder containing turmeric
- ½ cup red lentils
- 3 cups vegetable stock
- 1 can reduced-fat coconut milk

How to prepare:

1. Heat 1 tbsp olive oil in a cooking pot and add all the vegetables.
2. Sauté for about 5 minutes then add all the remaining ingredients.
3. Boil the soup then reduce the heat.
4. Cover the lid and cook for about 18 minutes.
5. Puree the soup using a handheld blender.
6. Garnish with herbs.
7. Serve warm.

Preparation time: 10 minutes
Cooking time: 25minutes
Total time: 35 minutes
Servings: 04

Nutritional Values:

- Calories 104
- Total Fat 3.7 g
- Saturated Fat 0.7 g
- Cholesterol 0 mg
- Total Carbs 26.5 g
- Sugar 1.4 g
- Fiber 0.7 g
- Sodium 141 mg
- Protein 5.4 g

APPETIZER RECIPES

Zucchini Pizza Bites

Ingredients:
- 4 slices large zucchini, cut ¼ inch thick
- Spray olive oil
- Pepper
- 4 tablespoons pizza sauce
- 2 tablespoons shredded part-skim mozzarella cheese

How to prepare:
1. Set the oven broiler to 500 degrees F.
2. Season the zucchini slices with pepper and olive oil.
3. Place in the slices on a baking sheet and broil them for 2 minutes.
4. Top each zucchini slice with pizza sauce and cheese.
5. Broil for another 2 minutes.
6. Serve warm.

Preparation time: 5 minutes
Cooking time: 5 minutes

Total time: 10 minutes
Servings: 04

Nutritional Values:

- Calories 201
- Total Fat 24.5 g
- Saturated Fat 3.7 g
- Cholesterol 151 mg
- Sodium 514 mg
- Total Carbs 9.3 g
- Fiber 1.3 g
- Sugar 0 g
- Protein 3.9 g

Two Tomato Bruschetta

Ingredients:

- 1/2 whole-grain baguette, cut into six 1/2-inch-thick diagonal slices
- 2 tablespoons chopped basil
- 1 tablespoon chopped parsley
- 2 cloves garlic, minced
- 3 tomatoes, diced
- 1/2 cup diced fennel
- 1 teaspoon olive oil
- 2 teaspoons balsamic vinegar
- 1 teaspoon black pepper

How to prepare:

1. Spread the baguette slices over a baking sheet.
2. Cook the slices in the oven at 370 degrees F until golden brown.
3. Mix the remaining ingredients in a bowl.

4. Top the baked banquette slices with this mixture.
5. Serve.

Preparation time: 10 minutes
Cooking time: 10 minutes
Total time: 20 minutes
Servings: 4

Nutritional Values:
- Calories 209
- Total Fat 10.5 g
- Saturated Fat 1.7 g
- Cholesterol 8 mg
- Sodium 663 mg
- Total Carbs 19.9 g
- Fiber 1.7 g
- Sugar 0.4 g
- Protein 9.3 g

Pumpkin Pie Spiced Yogurt

Ingredients:
- 2 cups low fat plain yogurt
- ½ cup pumpkin puree
- ¼ teaspoon cinnamon
- ¼ teaspoon pumpkin pie spice
- ¼ cup walnuts, chopped
- Honey or another sweetener, drizzle (optional)

How to prepare:
1. Combine pumpkin puree with all the spices and yogurt in a bowl.
2. Serve with honey and walnuts on top.
3. Serve.

Preparation time: 05 minutes
Cooking time: 0 minutes

Total time: 5 minutes
Servings: 2

Nutritional Values:
- Calories 167
- Total Fat 9.8 g
- Saturated Fat 1.4 g
- Cholesterol 20 mg
- Sodium 119 mg
- Total Carbs 11.3 g
- Fiber 0.5 g
- Sugar 1.2 g
- Protein 7.6 g

Fruit Skewers and Yogurt Dip

Ingredients:

Yogurt Dip
- 1 ½ cups non-fat Greek yogurt
- 8 ounces non-fat or low-fat cream cheese
- ¼ cup honey

Fruit Skewers
- 10 bamboo skewers
- 10-strawberries
- 20-blueberries
- 1-pineapple, cored and cubed
- 3-kiwis, peeled and cubed

How to prepare:
1. Thread all the fruits cubes in the skewers alternatively.
2. Mix all the ingredients for yogurt dip in a bowl.
3. Serve the skewers with yogurt dip.

Preparation time: 10 minutes
Cooking time: 0 minutes
Total time: 10 minutes
Servings: 6

Nutritional Values:
- Calories 181
- Total Fat 1.1 g
- Saturated Fat 0 g
- Cholesterol 0 mg
- Sodium 45 mg
- Total Carbs 17.1 g
- Fiber 1.1 g
- Sugar 5.3 g
- Protein 4.2 g

Crispy Garbanzo Beans

Ingredients:

- 2 cans (15 ounces) unsalted garbanzo beans
- ½ teaspoon salt
- ½ teaspoon pepper
- 1 teaspoon garlic powder
- 1 teaspoon onion powder
- 1 teaspoon dried parsley flakes
- 2 teaspoon dried dill
- Cooking spray

How to prepare:

1. Preheat oven to 400 degrees F.
2. Rinse and drain all the garbanzo beans. Remove all the excess water out them.
3. Mix all the remaining ingredient in a bowl.
4. Toss in garbanzo beans and mix well to coat.

5. Spread the beans on a greased baking sheet.
6. Place it on the lowest rack of the oven.
7. Roast the beans for about 30 to 40 minutes until golden brown.
8. Give a gentle stir after every 15 minutes.
9. Serve.

Preparation time: 10 minutes
Cooking time: 40 minutes
Total time: 50 minutes
Servings: 04

Nutritional Values:
- Calories 218
- Total Fat 4.7g
- Saturated Fat 1.6 g
- Cholesterol 30 mg
- Sodium 654 mg
- Total Carbs 31.9 g
- Fiber 0.5 g
- Sugar 0.7 g
- Protein 5.6 g

Ingredients:

- 1 15-ounce can beets
- 1 cup cider vinegar
- 1/2 cup sugar
- 2 teaspoons salt
- 2 bay leaves
- 4 whole cloves
- 1 medium onion, sliced into rings
- 6 large eggs

How to prepare:

1. Mix beets liquid with cloves, bay leaves, sugar and vinegar in a saucepan.
2. Bring the mixture to a boil and mxi well to dissolve the sugar.
3. Pour this liquid in a deep bowl.
4. Add onions to the liquid and set it aside for 1 hour.

5. Place eggs in a saucepan and cover them with water.
6. Boil egg water then reduce the heat to simmer. Cook for 10 minutes.
7. Drain and rinse the eggs under cold water.
8. Peel each egg and transfer them to the onion liquid.
9. Cover the bowl and refrigerate for 24 hours.
10.   Drain the eggs and slice them in half.
11.   Serve.

Preparation time: 10 minutes
Cooking time: 15 minutes
Total time: 25 minutes
Servings: 4

Nutritional Values:
- Calories 183
- Total Fat 16.3 g
- Saturated Fat 3.5 g
- Cholesterol 142 mg
- Sodium 144 mg
- Total Carbs 2.3g
- Fiber 1.3 g
- Sugar 1.7 g
- Protein 12.3 g

Apple-Sauced Nachos

Ingredients:

- 1/2 teaspoon apple pie spice
- Non-stick cooking spray
- 1 teaspoon granulated sugar
- 2 apples, cored and sliced
- 2 (6- or 7-inch) wheat tortillas
- 1/2 cup water
- 1 tablespoon brown sugar
- 1 tablespoon golden raisins
- 1/2 teaspoon finely shredded orange peel

How to prepare:

1. Set your oven to 400 degrees.
2. Coat the tortillas with oil on both the sides.
3. Mix them with apple pie spice and sugar in a bowl.
4. Dice each tortilla into 6 wedges.

5. Spread the tortilla wedges on a baking sheet and bake for 10 minutes.
6. Meanwhile, mix all the remaining ingredients in a saucepan.
7. Let the sauce boil then reduce the heat.
8. Let it cook for about 10 minutes.
9. Enjoy tortillas with applesauce.

Preparation time: 10 minutes
Cooking time: 20 minutes
Total time: 30 minutes
Servings: 04

Nutritional Values:

- Calories 219
- Total Fat 6.4 g
- Saturated Fat 2.5 g
- Cholesterol 11 mg
- Sodium 338 mg
- Total Carbs 20.4 g
- Fiber 1.3 g
- Sugar 22g
- Protein 8.5g

DESSERT RECIPES:

Walnut Chocolate Chip Cookies

Ingredients:

- 2 cups rolled oats
- 1/2 cup all-purpose flour
- 1/2 cup whole-wheat pastry flour
- 1 teaspoon ground cinnamon
- 1/2 teaspoon baking soda
- 1/2 teaspoon salt
- 1/2 cup tahini
- 4 tablespoons unsalted butter, cut into pieces
- 2/3 cup granulated sugar
- 2/3 cup packed light brown sugar
- 1 large egg
- 1 large egg white
- 1 tablespoon vanilla extract
- 1 cup semisweet or bittersweet chocolate chips
- 1/2 cup chopped walnuts

How to prepare:

1. Set your oven to 350 degrees F

2. Layer 2 baking sheets with a parchment paper.
3. Mix oats with both the flours, baking soda, salt and cinnamon in a bowl.
4. Beat butter with tahini in an electric mixer.
5. Whisk in sugars and beat well.
6. Stir in eggs, egg whites, and vanilla while beating continuously.
7. Add oats mixture and mix well.
8. Fold in walnuts and chocolate chips.
9. Prepare cookie balls out of this dough and place them on the baking sheets.
10. Lightly press each ball using your finger.
11. Bake for 16 minutes until golden brown.
12. Allow them to cool for 2 minutes.
13. Serve.

Preparation time: 5 minutes
Cooking time: 16 minutes
Total time: 21 minutes
Servings: 06

Nutritional Values:
- Calories 228
- Total Fat 5.7 g
- Saturated Fat 2.7 g
- Cholesterol 15 mg
- Sodium 114 mg
- Total Carbs 12.4 g
- Fiber 0.2g
- Sugar 15 g
- Protein 9.1 g

Milk Chocolate Pudding

Ingredients:
- 3 tablespoons corn-starch
- 2 tablespoons cocoa powder
- 2 tablespoons sugar
- 1/8 teaspoon salt
- 2 cups non-fat milk
- 1/3 cup chocolate chips
- 1/2 teaspoon vanilla

How to prepare:
1. Mix corn-starch with sugar, salt, and cocoa powder in a saucepan.
2. Stir in milk and cook on medium heat until it thickens.
3. Turn off the heat then fold in chocolate chips and vanilla.
4. Mix until well combined.
5. Divide the pudding into serving glasses.

6. Allow them to chill.

7. Serve.

Preparation time: 10 minutes
Cooking time: 5 minutes
Total time: 15 minutes
Servings: 2

Nutritional Values:
- Calories 349
- Total Fat 11.9 g
- Saturated Fat 1.7 g
- Cholesterol 78 mg
- Sodium 79 mg
- Total Carbs 8.8 g
- Fiber 1.1 g
- Sugar 10.3 g
- Protein 13 g

Pear-Strawberry Trifle

Ingredients:

- 2 pared, cored, and thinly sliced pears
- 2 tablespoons lemon juice
- 2 cups coarsely chopped strawberries
- ½ teaspoon almond extract, optional
- 2 tablespoons orange juice
- 2 tablespoons honey
- ½ 9 inch angel food cake, cut to 1-inch cubes
- 3 cups vanilla or lemon flavored yogurt

How to prepare:

1. Mix pears with lemon juice, almond extract, and strawberries in a bowl.
2. Whisk honey with orange juice in another bowl.

3. Layer each serving glass with a layer of 1/3 cake, 1 tablespoon orange juice mixture, 1 cup yogurt, 1 cup pear and 1 cup strawberries.
4. Top each glass with remaining yogurt.
5. Refrigerate for 1 to 2 hours.
6. Garnish with strawberries.
7. Serve.

Preparation time: 10 minutes
Cooking time: 0 minutes
Total time: 10 minutes
Servings: 2

Nutritional Values:
- Calories 321
- Total Fat 10.2 g
- Saturated Fat 4.4 g
- Cholesterol 120 mg
- Sodium 176 mg
- Total Carbs 19 g
- Fiber 1.9 g
- Sugar 21.4 g
- Protein 12.8 g

Carrot Cake Cookies

Ingredients:

- 1/2 cup applesauce
- 1/2 cup brown sugar
- 1/2 cup sugar
- 1/2 cup oil
- 2 eggs
- 1 teaspoon vanilla
- 1 cup flour
- 1 cup whole wheat flour
- 1 teaspoon baking soda
- 1 teaspoon baking powder
- 1/4 teaspoon salt
- 1 teaspoon ground cinnamon
- 1/2 teaspoon ground nutmeg
- 1/2 teaspoon ground ginger
- 2 cups old-fashioned rolled oats

- 1 1/2 cups finely grated carrots
- 1 cup raisins or golden raisins

How to prepare:
1. Set your oven to 350 degrees F.
2. Mix applesauce with eggs, oil, sugars, and vanilla in a bowl.
3. Stir in all the dry ingredients.
4. Mix well then fold in carrots and raisins.
5. Drop a tablespoon of cookie dough on the cookie sheet.
6. Add more cookies drop by drop.
7. Bake the cookies 15 minutes until golden brown in colour.
8. Serve

Preparation time: 10 minutes
Cooking time: 15 minutes
Total time: 25 minutes
Servings: 6

Nutritional Values:
- Calories 313
- Total Fat 24g
- Saturated Fat 18 g
- Cholesterol 61 mg
- Sodium 562 mg
- Total Carbs 23 g
- Fiber 1.7 g
- Sugar 39 g
- Protein 11 g

Fabulous Fig Bars

Ingredients:

- 16 ounces stemmed, chopped dried figs
- ½ cup chopped walnuts
- 1/3 cup sugar
- ¼ cup orange juice
- 2 tablespoons hot water
- ½ cup margarine softened
- 1 cup packed brown sugar
- 1 large egg
- 1 ½ cups all-purpose flour
- ½ teaspoon baking soda
- 1 ¼ cups old-fashioned rolled oat

How to prepare:

1. Set the oven to 350 degrees F. Grease a 9x13 inch baking pan.
2. Mix figs with sugar, walnuts, hot water and orange juice in a bowl.

3. Beat brown sugar with margarine in an electric mixer until creamy.
4. Whisk in egg and blend until smooth.
5. Stir in baking soda and flour. Mix well.
6. Add oats and mix well. Reserve 1 cup of the cookie dough for topping.
7. Transfer the remaining dough to the baking pan and press it gently.
8. Top the dough with figs mixture and press it firmly into the dough.
9. Sprinkle the reserved cookie dough on it.
10. Bake for about 30 minutes.
11. Slice into small squares.
12. Serve.

Preparation time: 10 minutes
Cooking time: 30 minutes
Total time: 40 minutes
Servings: 06

Nutritional Values:

- Calories 266
- Total Fat 4.9 g
- Saturated Fat 4.1 g
- Cholesterol 11 mg
- Sodium 13 mg
- Total Carbs 19.3 g
- Fiber 1.9 g
- Sugar 9.7 g
- Protein 3.4 g

Cranberry Apple Dessert Risotto

Ingredients:
- ½ cup dried cranberries
- 3 ½ cups fat-free milk
- 1 cinnamon stick
- 1 pinch salt
- 1 tablespoon butter
- 1 large golden apple, peeled, cored, and finely diced
- ½ cup Arborio rice
- 1 ½ cups apple cider
- 2 tablespoons packed light brown sugar

How to prepare:
1. Mix cranberries with boiling water in a bowl. Set it aside for 30 minutes.
2. Heat milk with salt and cinnamon stick in a microwave.
3. Cover the lid and set it aside.

4. Heat 1 tbsp butter in a large pot and add apple. Sauté for 2 minutes.
5. Stir in rice and cook for 30 seconds.
6. Add apple cider and cook until it is completely absorbed.
7. Whisk in sugar and mix well.
8. Add a half cup of the milk mixture and cook for 3 minutes.
9. Stir in another half cup milk and cook more.
10.   Continue cooking until entire milk is used.
11.   Discard cinnamon sticks.
12.   Serve.

Preparation time: 10 minutes
Cooking time: 20 minutes
Total time: 30 minutes
Servings: 4

Nutritional Values:
- Calories 291
- Total Fat 9.7 g
- Saturated Fat 8.6 g
- Cholesterol 121 mg
- Sodium 123 mg
- Total Carbs 27.1 g
- Fiber 0.9 g
- Sugar 11.3 g
- Protein 5.2 g

Ingredients:

- ⅔ cup plain low-fat kefir
- 1 tablespoon mini dark chocolate chips
- 1 tablespoon shredded unsweetened coconut
- ½ cup frozen, unsweetened yogurt, softened

How to prepare:

1. Add kefir to the serving glasses.
2. Top it with frozen yogurt.
3. Garnish with chocolate chips, coconuts, and fruits.
4. Serve.

Preparation time: 10 minutes
Cooking time: 30 minutes

Total time: 0 minutes
Servings: 2

Nutritional Values:

- Calories 178
- Total Fat 16 g
- Saturated Fat 4.2 g
- Cholesterol 2.1 mg
- Sodium *14 mg*
- Total Carbs 13.8 g
- Fiber 3.2 g
- Sugar 24.9 g
- Protein 7.2g

14 Day Meal Plan:

Day 1

Breakfast: Sweet Millet Congee

Snack: 1 Medium Apple

Lunch: Roasted Chicken Dal

Snack: Apple-sauced Nachos

Dinner: Asian Beef and Noodles

Day 2

Breakfast: Strawberry Breakfast Sandwich

Snack: 1 Medium Banana.

Lunch: Broiled Halibut with Tangy Yogurt Sauce

Snack: 1/2 cup Peaches

Dinner: White Bean and Chicken Chili

Day 3

Breakfast: Spinach Mushroom Feta Cheese Scramble

Snack: 1 Medium Orange.

Lunch: Red Bean Soup

Snack: 1/2 cup Pineapple.

Dinner: Mexican Bake

Dessert: Walnut Chocolate Chip Cookies

Day 4

Breakfast: Overnight Oatmeal

Snack: 1 Medium Banana.

Lunch: Chicken Kabobs

Snack: Pickled Eggs

Dinner: Apricot Spinach Quinoa

Day 5

Breakfast: Turkey Sausage and Mushroom Strata

Snack: 1 Medium Apple.

Lunch: Spice-rubbed Chicken

Snack: 1 cup of Fruit Salad.

Dinner: Tomato Pappardelle

Day 6

Breakfast: Millet Congee

Snack: 1 Medium Apple.

Lunch: Cauliflower Veggie Burger

Snack: 1/2 cup Mixed Berries

Dinner: Balsamic Chicken

Day 7

Breakfast: Veggie Quiche Muffins

Snack: 1 medium Pear.

Lunch: Crusted Pork Tenderloin

Snack: Pumpkin Pie Spiced Yogurt

Dinner: Smoked Mackerel and Orange Couscous

Dessert: Pear Strawberry Trifle

Day 8

Breakfast: Fruit n Grain Breakfast Salad

Snack: 1 Medium Apple

Lunch: Beef Kabobs with Grilled Pineapple Salsa

Snack: Fruit Skewers with Yogurt Dip

Dinner: Curried Squash, Lentil, and Coconut Soup

Day 9

Breakfast: Turkey sausage and Mushroom Strata

Snack: 1 Medium Banana.

Lunch: Garlic Lime Marinated Pork Chops

Snack: 1/2 cup Peaches

Dinner: Pesto Shrimp Skewers

Day 10

Breakfast: Veggies Quiche Muffins

Snack: 1 medium orange.

Lunch: Pork Medallions with Pear-Maple Sauce

Snack: Zucchini Pizza Bites

Dinner: Spicy Seafood Stew

Day 11

Breakfast: Overnight Oatmeal

Snack: 1 Medium Banana.

Lunch: Vegetable and Beef Skillet

Snack: 1/2 cup Pears

Dinner: Curried Vegetable Couscous

Dessert: Carrots Cake Cookies

Day 12

Breakfast: Spinach, Mushroom and Feta Cheese Scramble

Snack: 1 Medium Apple.

Lunch: Ginger Chicken with Rice Noodles

Snack: 1 cup of Fruit Salad.

Dinner: Shrimp Pasta Primavera

Day 13

Breakfast: Strawberry Breakfast Sandwich

Snack: 1 Medium Apple.

Lunch: Creole Turkey Meatballs

Snack: Two Tomato Bruschetta

Dinner: Mediterranean Vegetables

Dessert: Low-fat Chocolate Pudding.

Day 14

Breakfast: Millet Congee

Snack: 1 Medium Pear.

Lunch: Beef Stew

Snack: Crispy Garbanzo Beans

Dinner: Poached Salmon with Dill Sauce

Dessert: Coconut & Dark Chocolate Kefir Parfait

Conclusion

With the basic aim of creating a basic understanding of DASH diet, the length of this book covered various aspects of the diet from the very basics to its health benefits, its relation to various diseases, and the studies which led to the formulation of this dietary plan. Along with all this insight, a number of delicious and DASH suitable recipes are also added to the chapters. The 14-day meal plan is also there to the help all the beginners to give a better kick start to their DASH routine.

CPSIA information can be obtained
at www.ICGtesting.com
Printed in the USA
FFHW010828181218
49925671-54548FF